11/13/07 - gift 20.-

The Christmas Story

According to the Gospels of Matthew and Luke
From the King James Bible

Paintings by Gennady Spirin

Henry Holt and Company

New York

Henry Holt and Company, Inc., *Publishers since 1866*, 115 West 18th Street, New York, New York 10011

Henry Holt is a registered trademark of Henry Holt and Company, Inc.

Illustrations copyright © 1998 by Gennady Spirin. All rights reserved.

Published in Canada by Fitzhenry & Whiteside Ltd., 195 Allstate Parkway, Markham, Ontario L3R 4T8.

Library of Congress Cataloging-in-Publication Data

Bible, N.T. Matthew. English. Authorized. Selections. 1998.

The Christmas story: according to the Gospels of Matthew and Luke from

the King James Version / paintings by Gennady Spirin.

Presents the story of the birth of Christ, from Mary's meeting with the angel Gabriel to

the birth of baby Jesus in a stable and the visit of the shepherds and three Wise Men.

1. Jesus Christ—Nativity—Biblical teaching. [1. Jesus Christ—Nativity. 2. Bible—Selections. 3. Christmas.]

I. Spirin, Gennadii, ill. II. Bible N.T. Luke. English. Authorized. Selections. 1998. III. Title.

BT 315.A3 1998 232.92—dc21 97-50417

ISBN 0-8050-5292-5 / First Edition—1998

Designed by Martha Rago

The artist used tempera, watercolor, and pencil on watercolor paper to create the illustrations for this book.

Printed in Italy

3 5 7 9 10 8 6 4 2

For my godchildren

—G.S.

The Gospels are four books that tell the life of Christ and his teachings. They are found in the New Testament of the Bible.

⁓

The Gospel of Saint Matthew comes first, followed by the Gospels of Saints Mark, Luke, and John.

Saint Luke tells the story of the angel Gabriel's visit to Mary with the news that she would give birth to Jesus. Luke also tells about the journey to Bethlehem, the birth of Jesus in a stable, and the visit by the shepherds.

Most scholars believe that Luke was a physician. Some say he was also a painter. He traveled around the ancient world with Saint Paul, spreading the teachings of Christ. Many think Luke wrote his Gospel while living in Greece or Asia Minor seventy to eighty years after Christ's death and resurrection. He is considered to be the author of another book in the New Testament, the Acts of the Apostles. Of the four Gospel writers, he provides the most complete account of the circumstances of Christ's birth.

Matthew was one of Jesus' disciples. It is likely he wrote his Gospel fifty to seventy-five years after Christ's death and resurrection. Matthew believed that the birth of Jesus fulfilled a prophecy in the Old Testament: "Behold, a virgin shall be with child, and shall bring forth a son, and they shall call his name Emmanuel, which being interpreted is, God with us" (Matthew 1:23). Matthew's Gospel provides the story of the three wise men. Like Luke, Matthew traveled to many places in the ancient world and preached about Jesus.

AND IN THE SIXTH month the angel Gabriel was sent from God unto a city of Galilee, named Nazareth,

To a virgin espoused to a man whose name was Joseph, of the house of David; and the virgin's name was Mary.

And the angel came in unto her, and said, Hail, thou that art highly favored, the Lord is with thee: blessed art thou among women.

And when she saw him, she was troubled at his saying, and cast in her mind what manner of salutation this should be.

And the angel said unto her, Fear not, Mary: for thou hast found favor with God.

And, behold, thou shalt conceive in thy womb, and bring forth a son, and shalt call his name Jesus.

He shall be great, and shall be called the Son of the Highest: and the Lord God shall give unto him the throne of his father David:

And he shall reign over the house of Jacob for ever; and of his kingdom there shall be no end.

Then said Mary unto the angel, How shall this be, seeing I know not a man?

And the angel answered and said unto her, The Holy Ghost shall come upon thee, and the power of the Highest shall overshadow thee: therefore also that holy thing which shall be born of thee shall be called the Son of God.

And Mary said, Behold the handmaid of the Lord; be it unto me according to thy word. And the angel departed from her.

II

Then Joseph her husband, being a just man, and not willing to make her a public example, was minded to put her away privily.

But while he thought on these things, behold, the angel of the Lord appeared unto him in a dream, saying, Joseph, thou son of David, fear not to take unto thee Mary thy wife: for that which is conceived in her is of the Holy Ghost.

And she shall bring forth a son, and thou shalt call his name Jesus: for he shall save his people from their sins.

Then Joseph being raised from sleep did as the angel of the Lord had bidden him, and took unto him his wife.

13

14

And it came to pass in those days, that there went out a decree from Caesar Augustus, that all the world should be taxed.

And all went to be taxed, every one into his own city.

And Joseph also went up from Galilee, out of the city of Nazareth, into Judaea, unto the city of David, which is called Bethlehem (because he was of the house and lineage of David),

To be taxed with Mary his espoused wife, being great with child.

And so it was, that, while they were there, the days were accomplished that she should be delivered.

And she brought forth her firstborn son, and wrapped him in swaddling clothes, and laid him in a manger; because there was no room for them in the inn.